MAKING
MOSAICS

By
**EDMOND
ARVOIS**

STERLING PUBLISHING CO., INC.
NEW YORK

Oak Tree Press Co., Ltd.
London & Sydney

STERLING CRAFTS BOOKS

Cardboard Crafting

Carpentry for Children

Ceramics—and How to Decorate Them

Complete Crayon Book

Creating from Scrap

Creative Claywork

Creative Enamelling & Jewelry-Making

Creative Leathercraft

Creative Paper Crafts in Color

Designs—And How to Use Them

Etching (and Other Intaglio Techniques)

How to Make Things Out of Paper

Make Your Own Mobiles

Making Mosaics

Original Creations with Papier Mâché

Papier Mâché—and How to Use It

Plastic Foam for Arts and Crafts

Prints—from Linoblocks and Woodcuts

Sculpture for Beginners

Stained Glass Crafting

Tin-Can Crafting

Types of Typefaces

Weaving as a Hobby

PICTURE CREDITS

Photographs on the following pages are from The Metropolitan Museum of Art: page 71, Gift of J. Pierpont Morgan, 1917; page 72, Gift of Mrs. W. Bayard Cutting, 1932; page 74, Purchase, 1938, Joseph Pulitzer Bequest.

Other photographs: pages 73, 81, Turkish Information Office; pages 76, 77, 79, 80, 83, Italian State Tourist Office.

Sixth Printing, 1971

Copyright © 1964 by Sterling Publishing Co., Inc.
419 Park Avenue South, New York, N.Y. 10016
British edition published by Oak Tree Press Co., Ltd., Nassau, Bahamas
Distributed in Australia by Oak Tree Press Co., Ltd.,
P.O. Box 34, Brickfield Hill, Sydney 2000, N.S.W.
Distributed in the United Kingdom and elsewhere in the British Commonwealth
by Ward Lock Ltd., 116 Baker Street, London W 1

Translated by Leonard F. Wise and adapted by Robert F. Scott from the original French edition, copyright 1963 (Editions J. Jacobs, Paris), which was based in part upon *Mosaik som hobby*, by C. Larssen (Jul. Gjellerups Forlag, Copenhagen).

Manufactured in the United States of America
All rights reserved
Library of Congress Catalog Card No.: 64-15109
ISBN 0-8069-5060-9   UK 7061 2019 1
5061-7

The ultimate in mosaics:
*A mosaic applied to a
piece of statuary.*

Contents

CONTENTS (continued)

Before You Begin

The mosaic, one of the oldest of the art forms, is today enjoying a resurgence of interest and for good reason. Using simple and widely available materials, it is possible with mosaics to create objects of beauty and practicality.

As the title indicates, this is a book that tells you how to make mosaics. You will immediately set to work making mosaics as you are introduced to the materials and methods of mosaics. The projects start with simple and useful objects and progress through mosaics of increasing complexity. For readers who may not be near a source of supply of the traditional mosaic materials, one section of the book is devoted to the use of unusual materials in mosaics, including detailed instructions on the making and coloring of mosaic stones.

Each project is described in clear and easily-followed language, giving the exact procedures for making practical and decorative objects of lasting beauty, while photographs and diagrams illustrate the steps to be followed. There is no aspect of the hobby kit or paint-by-number technique in this book. Emphasis is placed on improvisation in the use of materials at hand, and you are encouraged to set out in new directions and to explore the use of new and unusual materials. This is a book that will bring all of your creative energies into play, and perhaps will challenge you to discover the many sides of the art of the mosaic.

Illus. 1. This simple gravel mosaic design has been framed as a
picture to decorate a child's room.

Making Mosaics

A mosaic is traditionally the creation of a design or a picture by a combination of components—often of odd and multi-colored shapes—laid on a base and embedded in a material which serves to hold them and which may also fill the spaces between the pieces.

To make a mosaic you need:

a design to reproduce

pieces of some material with which to form the mosaic

a base

an adhesive and/or a cementing medium

A mosaic can be made using almost any material. To demonstrate this, try the following project:

MAKE A GRAVEL MOSAIC

Materials Checklist
small china or plastic bowl or dessert dish
colored cord or round laces, black or brown
light-colored gravel
crayon
household glue or contact cement

The light-colored gravel can be obtained from a beach or sand pit. You might even be lucky to discover that there are shades of lighter or darker gravel available near your home.

Sketch with crayon a simple design of random or free-form shapes on the bowl or dessert dish. Using ordinary household glue or contact cement, apply the cord or round laces to the design following the outline and cutting the cord or laces when necessary. This will mark the edges of your mosaic design. Now, covering one area enclosed by edging at a time, lay a coating of glue or contact cement on the surface of the dish. While it is still wet, sprinkle gravel evenly over the cement-covered area and shake off the excess. (If you were lucky enough to find vari-colored gravels, you can alternate the colors from area to area on the surface of the dish.) Repeat this process with adjoining areas until the entire surface of the dish is covered with fine gravel. Using water-colors or tempera colors, you can color each area separately later if you want more color contrast.

TIP: In this and in all other mosaic projects to come, be sure to let your adhesive or cement dry well after laying the mosaic. Do not be in a hurry; be patient! Many a project has been spoiled because of failure to let the adhesive or cement dry thoroughly.

When dry, your bowl will mark the completion of your first mosaic project. You will be pleased at the interesting effect created by the rough texture of the gravel and the composition of the shapes and colors you have created.

Using colored cord or laces and gravel, you can similarly decorate book ends, lamp bases and other objects.

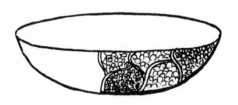

Illus. 2. *A bowl with a gravel mosaic makes an ideal nut dish.*

Adhesives

The purpose of adhesives in mosaic-making is to form a bond—either temporary or permanent—between the pieces of the mosaic and the base.

Temporary adhesives include wallpaper paste (you can make an excellent temporary paste by mixing flour and water—but be sure to mix it thoroughly to remove the lumps), library paste and rubber cement. Rubber cement has two advantages—any excess can be removed when dry by rubbing, and when it is applied to only a single surface, the bond is not permanent (the object can be lifted and moved), but when rubber cement is applied to both surfaces to be joined, an almost permanent bond is achieved.

More-permanent adhesives include old-fashioned mucilage, transparent (model aircraft) cement, contact cement, hoof or hide glue (such as is used by furniture makers), mastic (employed in mounting plastic or cork floor tile), the newer polyvinyl resins and—the most permanent of all—epoxy cement. The latter comes in two tubes or jars, one the cement and the other the hardener. Epoxy cement should only be mixed immediately before use and then only in small quantities.

MAKE A PAPER MOSAIC ON A BOX TOP

Materials Checklist
small wooden box
colored cardboard or blotting paper (black, white, red)
rubber cement

This is an excellent project for transforming a plain wooden box into an attractive desk container for paper clips or trinkets.

Illus. 3. You can keep chessmen in this box with a mosaic top that doubles as a playing board.

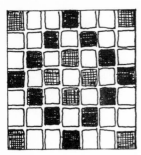

The object is to decorate the box top with a simple and pleasing geometric design. First, carefully cement a sheet of white cardboard on the box top, making sure there are no bubbles, wrinkles or raised places. It must completely cover the box top. Depending upon the size of the top, rule the red and black sheets into squares measuring $\frac{3}{8}''$, $\frac{1}{2}''$ or $\frac{3}{4}''$. If the top is square and large enough to accommodate 8 squares about $1''$ on a side in each direction, alternate the red and black squares. (A red square must be in each lower right-hand corner.) The resulting box will make an excellent container for chess pieces, and the top can serve as a playing board.

Your determination of the size of the squares will require some care so as to make the paper squares fit from edge to edge. A thin strip of white should be left between squares as they are pasted down. Some suggested designs are shown in the margin.

Although it is of paper, the design that you have created is nonetheless a mosaic. In making this project, you have encountered some of the problems that you will be called upon to solve in later projects involving other materials.

Mosaic Stones

Tesserae (the word, of Latin derivation, originally came from the Greek word *tesseragonos*, meaning 'four-cornered') may be mosaic "stones" of various materials and even natural stone itself. The most common of the natural mosaic stones are marble, agate, and onyx. Although some craftsmen still use natural stones, most mosaics are now made with materials created specifically for the mosaicist. These materials may be classified as follows:

Glass tile, measuring about ¾″ by ¾″ (20 mm. by 20 mm.), often called Venetian glass tile because it was first made in Venice. It comes pasted on sheets of paper about a foot square or in bulk form by the pound, in single or assorted colors. This tile is moulded and is therefore quite uniform in size. The range of available colors is moderate.

Glass tile, measuring about ⅜″ by ½″ (10 mm. by 15 mm.), is often called "smalti tipo antico" or Byzantine tile. This tile is similar to that used in the famous mosaics of Ravenna and Constantinople. It is made in large sheets and then split by machine; the surfaces are often slightly irregular but this increases the reflective qualities of the tile. It is sold in bulk form only. The range of available colors is large. These smaller tiles are, of course, more adaptable for use in decorating small objects.

Ceramic tile, measuring about ¾″ by ¾″ (20 mm. by 20 mm.), made of clay with a colored glaze. It comes pasted face down on sheets of paper or face up on sheets of open-weave fabric. It is also sold in

Venetian

Byzantine

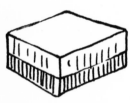

Glazed ceramic

Illus. 4. *You will soon learn to recognize the different kinds of tesserae.*

bulk form by the pound in single or assorted colors. The range of available colors is moderate. Colored unglazed ceramic tile may also be found.

Porcelain tile, measuring about ⅜″ by ⅜″ (10 mm. by 10 mm.). The range of available colors is limited. Like the Byzantine tiles, the smaller porcelain tiles are also more suitable for mosaic decoration of small objects.

Glazed ceramic tiles are also available in shapes known as "brick tile" which are sold in foot-square sheets containing assorted sizes: ⅜″ by ⅜″; ⅜″ by ⅝″; and ⅝″ by ⅝″. Other varieties include foot-square sheets of glazed ceramic tiles shaped like leaves of various sizes (leaf tile) and random shapes and sizes (pebble tile) sold in foot-square sheets and in bulk bags.

Note that the Venetian glass or the glazed ceramic or porcelain tesserae are more desirable for making a mosaic on a surface that should be flat, as for example, a table top. The irregularities of the Byzantine tesserae make them less desirable for this purpose.

Other tiles or materials that should not be overlooked by mosaicists include small pieces of stained glass such as used by the makers of stained-glass windows; colored ceramic bathroom tile (often called tapestry tile), which measures 4¼″ by 4¼″ but can be broken up or cut into smaller sizes and shapes; and various decorative plastic tile materials.

Although the tiles you buy may be pasted on paper when you get them, it will be best for you to remove them from their backing before using. They can be removed by soaking the tiles and backing material in warm water for a short time.

Mosaic materials can usually be purchased at hobby, handicraft or art supply stores, but half the fun of making mosaics will be in finding new materials yourself. Flattened and well-smoothed beach or stream pebbles make attractive mosaic material, especially if dark-colored and set off against a light background or vice versa.

MAKE A HOT PLATE OR TRIVET

Materials Checklist
square of thin plywood or masonite
tesserae
permanent adhesive

Using the tesserae of your choice, you can now make a hot plate or trivet upon which you can set hot cooking utensils or dishes without damaging the surface of a dining table or other piece of fine furniture. Of course, when not in use it will make an attractive kitchen or dining room decoration.

Choose a small piece of thin ($\frac{1}{8}''$) plywood or masonite composition hardboard about 5" or 6" square. Have some additional baseboards handy—you will undoubtedly wish to make several of these practical and decorative hot plates at the same time.

Waterproof the baseboard with a coat or two of shellac. Shellac dries quickly, and two thin coats are better than one thick coat.

Illus. 5. A hot plate or trivet is a simple, useful project.

You may wish to rule off your mosaic design on a sheet of paper, indicating the tesserae as squares or rectangles of the appropriate size and shape. The spaces between tesserae can be shown as parallel lines spaced close together. In this way you can envisage what the design of your mosaic will look like before it is finished.

Cement the tesserae to the baseboard using a permanent-type adhesive. Then, using rubber cement, fix a piece of green felt the same size as the baseboard to the back to avoid marring the finish of any furniture upon which the hot plate is set. Leave the spaces between the stones open until you have read the next section; you can then fill in these interstices between stones with mosaic cement.

Mosaic Cements and Grouts

Up to now you have been using simple adhesives to affix your mosaic components to the bases. You can now create a mosaic more nearly resembling the great classical mosaics of antiquity through the use of mosaic cement and grout. In this book, the term "mosaic cement" will be used to describe the material (portland cement, tile cement, concrete, magnesite, plaster of Paris, etc.) which—under certain given circumstances—will serve as a bed and receive the pieces of the mosaic. The term "grout" will be reserved for a mixture having more water added to it than is usually added to mosaic cement. This you will use to fill the interstices between the component pieces of a mosaic—after the components have either been set in a bed of mosaic cement, or cemented directly to the base.

Hobby, handicraft or art supply stores all carry a variety of materials which are loosely called tile cement or grout. You can also buy portland cement in bags at your hardware supplier.

TIP: To "stretch" portland cement, mix it in the proportion of one part of portland cement to three parts of clean, medium-grained less-expensive sand. The sand-cement mixture should also be used on large mosaic projects, particularly those outdoor projects that will be exposed to the elements. This overcomes the tendency of pure portland cement to crack.

Portland cement is sold in two shades, grey and white. The grey cement is stronger, but the white cement can be more easily and more brightly dyed by the addition of water-soluble dyes to the mix or by the addition of ground pigments to the cement powder.

Cement does not set by "drying." Instead, cement should be "cured" by covering it with wet cloths or wet newspapers and allowing it to stand for several days until hard.

Still another mosaic cement material is magnesite, a non-waterproof cement used in flooring work. It has the advantage that setting time can be controlled and that it forms a close bond with wood or com-position hardboard mosaic bases, in contrast to the poor holding qualities of concrete. It can be purchased from flooring materials dealers. For small mosaics, fine-grained patching plaster (sometimes called "spackle") also makes an excellent mosaic cement or grouting material, and boxes of it can be obtained in paint shops.

Plaster of Paris is occasionally used by mosaicists (it is especially desirable if your mosaic is to be inset into an already existing plaster wall). However, ordinary plaster of Paris has the distinct disadvantage of having a very short setting time. This necessitates working quickly or working in very small areas at a time. This disadvantage can be overcome somewhat through the addition of various substances to retard the setting time. You can purchase "plaster retarder" at most paint or building materials suppliers. You can also use tartaric acid obtained from a chemical supply house. Or, you can add white vinegar to the plaster mix (substituting it for an equivalent quantity of water). Remember, however, that these substances, although retarding the setting time, tend to weaken the resultant plaster. They should be used sparingly.

The mosaic cement of your choice should be mixed to the consistency of modelling clay, following the directions of the supplier. Grout should have the consistency of heavy cream. It should be heavy enough to be worked by hand, but thin enough to penetrate into the interstices between the individual tesserae.

MAKE A CHEESE TRAY FROM A BREADBOARD

Materials Checklist
breadboard
tesserae
mosaic cement
sheet of green felt
rubber cement

If you have an old breadboard at home that has been replaced by a newer one, a mosaic-tile covering on it will convert it into an attractive cheese tray for the display and serving of fine cheeses.

Affix the tesserae that you have selected to the breadboard using a permanent adhesive. You may wish to sketch your design directly on the surface of the breadboard before laying down the individual stones. You can then fill in the spaces between the

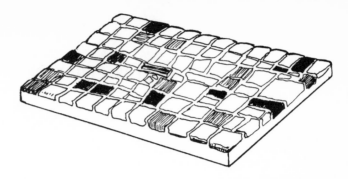

stones using a grout composed of a thin mixture of mosaic cement and water.

Illus. 6. This tray makes the serving of cheeses more appetizing.

You may want to touch up the mosaic cement in the spaces between the tesserae using a table knife. (A nutmeat pick also makes an excellent tool for this purpose.) Copper scouring pads from your kitchen will help to remove any excess mosaic cement from the surface of the mosaic. (Copper scouring pads are not as hard as steel wool pads; they are less likely to scratch the face of glass or ceramic tesserae.) A sponge should be used to remove the white powder that will be left after going over the mosaic with the copper scouring pad.

The edge of the breadboard can be stained with a contrasting wood stain to set off the color of your mosaic. Or you may wish to glue one row of tesserae along the edge of the breadboard to conceal completely the origins of the humble mosaic base that you used.

A layer of green felt, rubber-cemented to the underside of your cheese tray, will complete it and will prevent the marring or scratching of your furniture.

NOTE: If you wish, now is the time to add grout to the hot plates you made earlier. The grouted hot plate will be heavier and will serve as a better heat insulator.

Baseboards and Edging

Practically any stiff and fairly strong surface can support a mosaic. Some types of mosaic work (mosaics applied to walls, floors, or to objects like vases) require special handling, which will be discussed later. Initially, however, the beginner's problem will be mastering the technique of applying mosaics to relatively small horizontal surfaces.

You must keep in mind that the tesserae in a 36-inch square mosaic, depending on the nature of the mosaic materials used, may weigh as much as 20 pounds, to which must also be added the weight of the cement and of the baseboard itself. The choice of a baseboard, therefore, must be determined by the dimensions of the mosaic to be made and its eventual use.

The baseboard can be a stiff and fairly strong piece of cardboard, a metal plate, a sheet of plywood, a panel of composition hardboard like masonite, wallboard or even plain wood. The latter is generally undesirable unless it has been completely waterproofed and made impervious to moisture; for this reason, many mosaicists prefer the plywood (marine or exterior grade) or wood composition panels, but even these can stand a coat or two of waterproofing if they are to remain stable and free from warping effects.

The waterproofing materials can be any of the traditional materials used by painters for this purpose: Shellac makes an excellent waterproofing compound, particularly for porous materials, and it has the advantage of drying quickly. Varnish will do, too, although the drying time is longer. You may wish to use any one of a number of rubber-base waterproofing compounds so much used by home-owners. Or, you can use any left-over paint. The idea is to get a waterproof layer between your mosaic and the baseboard.

Square, rectangular, round, oval and free-form table tops in plywood or composition hardboard are now available in many stores specializing in do-it-yourself furniture components. These make ideal subjects for decoration with mosaics. Wrought-iron bases, brass tripods and table legs of various woods are also available for combining with the table top you select.

Illus. 7. An oval table with a mosaic of simple and pleasing design. The edging and the legs are of metal.

For the mosaicist who cannot find at home or in stores suitable furniture for mosaic application, there are book ends, lamp bases, snack and serving trays, jewel boxes and small wooden chests, cheese and cutting boards, and similar articles on which mosaics may be applied. These can be purchased at art supply or handicraft stores.

One comparatively unexplored area for the mosaicist would be the use of transparent materials (glass, plastic, plexiglass, etc.) for mosaic bases. Aside from their stability and the fact that they are unaffected by moisture, their transparency also recommends them. Try using a clear transparent adhesive to mount glass tesserae to a glass or plastic base and select two colors or two kinds of tesserae that will pass light in varying degrees. With these, you can create a colorful mosaic name plate or house-number plate, and you can even illuminate it at night!

For a baseboard to contain a mosaic and its mosaic cement, it needs some kind of border or edging.

TIP: Many mosaicists prefer to use a temporary border around a mosaic while it is in the process of being made. They mount the permanent border only after the messy work has been completed. In this way, there can be no early damage to the permanent border.

You might defer selecting and mounting a permanent border on a mosaic until you can find a border that provides an appropriate and harmonious color match.

Edgings may be of wood or metal, such as brass or aluminium. Among the wood materials available are wood strips and picture-frame materials. Metal edgings can be purchased in hardware stores or from handicraft shops. The aluminium strips and channels for edging formica-topped kitchen work tables and counter tops are ideal.

The height of the edging selected should be equal to the thickness of the mosaic material, the mortar bed and/or the baseboard. The most common width of edging, whether of wood or metal, is 1″. Thickness of standard wood edging is $\frac{1}{8}$″, while metal edgings will measure from 1/20″ (thin) through 1/10″ (medium) to $\frac{1}{8}$″ (thick) in thickness. For curved or round baseboards, the more easily bent metal edgings are preferred to wood edging.

A corner with the ends of the edging cut at angles of 45° always looks more attractive than a simple butt joint. If you anticipate doing much mosaic work requiring the cutting of borders, frames or edging materials, the purchase of a mitre box would be a wise investment. A mitre box holds both the work to be cut and the saw at the correct angle; perfect joints will result every time.

MAKE FLOWER STANDS AND TABLES

Illus. 8. This plant stand combines simplicity of mosaic design with clean lines to give a completely harmonious effect.

MAKE FLOWER STANDS AND TABLES

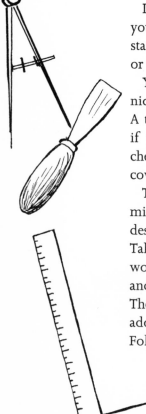

Materials Checklist
table top or piece of plywood or masonite
legs (purchased from furniture store)
        or
old table from your attic
waterproofing base coat
tesserae
permanent adhesive
mosaic cement
edging material

Depending upon the degree of your self-confidence, you can now attempt to mosaic the top of a simple stand for flower pots and vases, a small lamp table, or a larger or more elaborate coffee table.

You are now ready to put into practice the techniques you have learned in the preceding projects. A table-top mosaic presents no special problems, and if you have mastered the making of hot plates and cheese boards, you should have no difficulty in covering with a mosaic the table top you selected.

TIP: Remember that it is much easier to correct a mistake or an error in judgment on a preliminary design drawing than it is on the finished mosaic. Take care to make your measurements carefully. It would be embarrassing to complete your mosaic and discover you had made an error in measurement. There is an old carpenter's adage that should be adopted by mosaicists: Measure twice and cut once. Follow it and it will save you many headaches.

Tools and Nippers

Up until now you have been using the most primitive and still the most useful tools of all—your hands—to make mosaics. Undoubtedly you have already appropriated some useful kitchen utensils (knife, spatula) or tools from your workshop (long-nosed pliers, straightedge) to assist you in your projects. There are, however, some professional tools which will be useful now to add to your collection. These will make your working methods more professional.

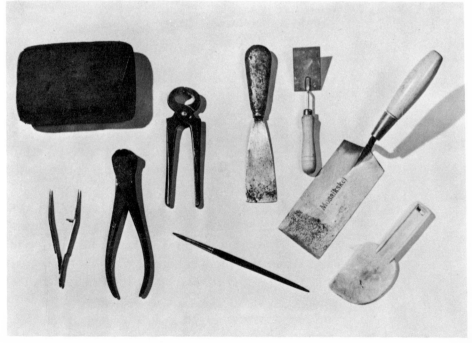

Illus. 9. The tools of the mosaicist.

These include:

a heavy cellulose sponge, for wiping away the excess grout from the faces of mosaics

a pair of tweezers, for holding tesserae while applying adhesive and for placing small tesserae in position on the base

a flexible-bladed scraper or putty knife, for forcing grout deeply and firmly into the interstices between tesserae

a plasterer's trowel, for applying and smoothing large areas of mosaic cement

a plastic scraper—the kind used to remove ice from the windshield of your car is excellent—for scraping excess grout or mosaic cement from the faces of the mosaic; a metal tool would scratch glass, porcelain or glazed ceramic tesserae

a small round-tipped paint brush, for applying water colors, touching up, etc.

cutting nippers, whose use will be explained now in detail.

If the table top that you selected in the preceding project was round, oval or of a free-form shape, it may have occurred to you that a more regular fit of square or rectangular tesserae could be achieved if they were cut in some fashion. Nippers, the kind used for cutting by professional mosaicists, will enable you to cut tesserae (including glass tesserae) to specific sizes and shapes and will give you a wider range of expression in your mosaics. The best nippers have carbide cutting edges. They cost a little bit more than ordinary nippers, but are well worth the difference, as they have a longer life and cut tesserae cleanly.

TIP: *Always* use goggles when cutting tesserae to protect your eyes from flying chips. They are not the mark of the amateur, for all professional mosaicists use them.

The technique of cutting tesserae is easily learned: Do not attempt to place the entire tile in the mouth of the nippers. Instead, use the side of the nippers to "bite" the stone as shown in Illustration 10. The edge of the cutters must lie in the same line as the cut you wish to make. You may spoil a few tiles or glass tesserae in the beginning, but with practice you will soon get the knack of cutting and be able to split off pieces of tile like an expert.

TIP: In choosing nippers, always select the pair with the longest handles. By holding the nippers near the ends of the handles, you will be able to cut more easily because of the better leverage.

Illus. 10. The right way to cut mosaic tiles with the nippers.

Illus. 11. Wiping off the finished mosaic inlaid in a cupboard door.

MAKE A CUPBOARD-DOOR INLAY

Materials Checklist
old cupboard or commode with recessed panel doors
permanent adhesive
tesserae
mosaic cement

By inlaying a mosaic in the recessed door or doors of a commode or cupboard, you can transform the appearance of an old piece of furniture into something new and different. Generally speaking, geometric or abstract designs are preferred for such purposes.

The procedure is simple. Remove the door or doors from the cupboard or commode by removing the screws on the cupboard side of the hinges. (Put the screws away carefully as you will need to put them back later.) Cement each of the tesserae into place individually. Then work grout into the interstices between the tesserae, levelling off the grout mixture before it has set too hard. No edging is necessary on such a mosaic; the higher edges of the panelled door serve as a border for the mosaic. Now replace the doors on your cupboard and step back and admire your handiwork.

Other Methods of Cutting Stones

There are several other ways in which to achieve smaller sizes or different shapes of tesserae, besides using cutting nippers. Some handicraft shops, for example, sell bags of tesserae, that have been broken in the process of manufacture. Buying these is an economical way of obtaining material if square or rectangular shapes are not required.

Whole tesserae can also be cut with a hammer with a sharp cutting edge, such as a brick-mason's hammer. You can hold the larger tiles or tesserae in your hand for cutting, but if you do, be sure to wear a heavy leather glove. The traditional method of cutting tesserae is with a chisel and mallet. You will need a heavy wooden mallet and a stone cutter's chisel. In the beginning it is probably advisable to do your cutting at the bottom of a cardboard carton—the sides will prevent the pieces of the tesserae from flying about and getting lost. A solid slab of wood will serve as an admirable block on which to cut.

Other tools that can be successfully used to cut tesserae, with which you can experiment, are diamond or carborundum cutting wheels. These can be attached to a small circular saw motor or drill chuck. The diamond blade, being harder, will have a considerably longer life.

A steel-wheel glass cutter, which can be purchased in a hardware store, is useful for cutting glass, ceramic or porcelain tesserae. Simply make an initial cut with the steel cutting wheel and then use the notched handle for breaking the tesserae. Such a glass cutter is also useful for cutting pieces of stained glass if you are using these in your mosaics.

In learning the technique of cutting, you should remember that pieces of tesserae that have not broken quite as you wanted them to need not be thrown away. Save them—you will always find a use for such pieces.

Still another method of cutting stones requires considerably more raw material: Place the tesserae between layers of newspaper or a heavy cloth (an old blanket) on a firm, flat surface and strike with a hammer. Only break stones of one color at a time. The random shapes that you get by this method cannot be duplicated in any other way. Of course, there is much wastage, too.

MAKE A TABLE-TOP INLAY

Materials Checklist

table top or piece of plywood or masonite
legs (purchased from furniture store)
      or
old table from your attic
piece of plywood to support mosaic in hole cut in table top
waterproofing base coat
tesserae
permanent adhesive
mosaic cement
edging material

You may some day wish to mosaic only a small portion of a table top, rather than the entire top. To do this it will be necessary to cut a hole in the top, in the size and shape you desire. Using wood screws, attach a piece of plywood or composition board larger than the hole to the underside of the table. This will be the baseboard for your mosaic panel or inlay; the sides of the hole that you have cut will serve as the edging and will serve to contain your mosaic. Give the board two coats of shellac, and do not forget the raw edges of the hole in the table top. (Be careful not to get any shellac on the surface of the table.)

Now fix the individual tesserae to the wood composition or plywood sheet using one of the permanent adhesives. When the assemblage is dry, fill in the interstices between tesserae with grout.

The shape of a mosaic should always fit in with the size, shape and general appearance of the piece of furniture being decorated with the mosaic. In the case of the table shown in the illustration, a round mosaic was the obvious shape to use. On a rectangular table, a right-angled shape with an asymmetrical or checkerboard pattern would be appropriate.

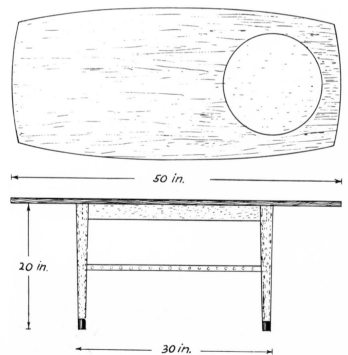

50 in.

20 in.

30 in.

Illus. 1 2. Details of construction and measurements of the table with inlaid mosaic top.

29

Illus. 13. (Left)
Assembling the mosaic
"in reverse" on a sheet
of paper ruled off to
represent the area to be
inlaid and the positions of
the individual tesserae.

Illus. 14. (Below) The
finished mosaic inlaid in
the table top. The mosaic
motif is a political map
of the western
hemisphere.

Finishing and Waxing

A completed mosaic, such as the inlaid table top just described, may risk having water, tea or other liquids spilled on it. Although portland cement is relatively impervious to most liquids, plaster of Paris, if untreated, quickly absorbs moisture. And almost all mosaic cement materials become easily stained by liquids that might spill upon them, unless steps have been taken to apply a finish to them.

To avoid unsightly staining of your finished mosaic, you have several choices of finishing techniques:

You can first clean the face of your mosaic using one of the prepared mosaic cleaners available in art supply and handicraft stores.

You can then coat the tesserae and the grout-filled spaces between the tesserae with a silicone preparation called "sealer," which is available at most handicraft stores. If your grouting cement was plaster of Paris, a very good finish would be to coat the entire mosaic with two thin coats of white shellac. (Two thin coats are always preferable to one thick coat for finishes.) Remember that shellac may take on a white "bloom" when wet; it is therefore not a good finish for a mosaic upon which drinks or other liquids may be set down or spilled. In such a case, use one of the synthetic varnishes available from the paint dealer. Whether you use sealer, shellac or varnish on your mosaic, you can always make the finish tougher and more durable by giving your mosaic a final coat of clear paste wax, followed by an energetic buffing.

MAKE AN ENTRANCE MOSAIC

Materials Checklist
marble or unglazed tile tesserae
portland cement

The foyer or entrance hallway of your home makes an excellent place for a mosaic. The water-repellent properties of tesserae make such a placement ideal— your mosaic cannot be damaged by dripping umbrellas or muddy overshoes.

Of course, glazed ceramic or porcelain tesserae

(continued on page 41)

Illus. 15. This mosaic in an entrance hall combines usefulness and beauty. A mosaic with a light background can lighten an otherwise dark corner of the house.

Illus. 16. Affixing mosaic stones to ruled paper with a temporary adhesive. A finished mosaic is in the background.

Illus. 17. Mosaic inlaid into the top of a rectangular table, giving a harmonious blending of wood grain and mosaic design.

Illus. 18. A panel of mosaic designs using $\frac{3}{4}''$ by $\frac{3}{4}''$ stones, $\frac{3}{8}''$ by $\frac{3}{8}''$ stones, rectangular tesserae and irregular shapes.

Illus. 19. One mosaicist's *Africa*: The giraffe and palm tree are effectively set off by the simple background.

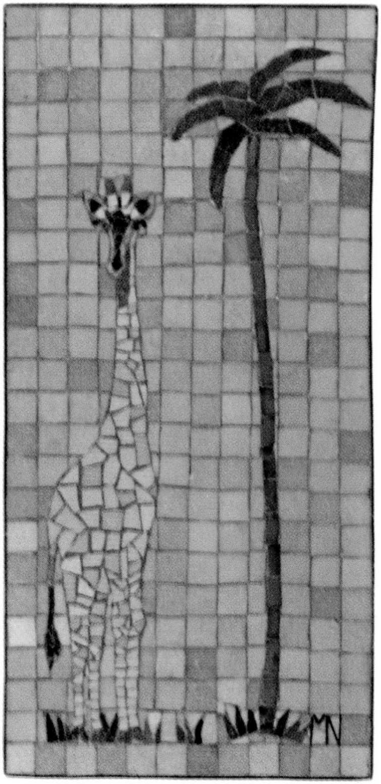

Illus. 20. A shallow ceramic dish with a single-color mosaic applied to the inside. Note the effect achieved by the mosaicist in utilizing the natural tone of the outside of the dish for contrast.

Illus. 21. (Above) A contemporary mosaic: The Singing Lesson.

Illus. 23. (Above) A striking use of color and design in a round table top.

Illus. 22. (Left page, bottom) A fish motif serves as an inviting subject for a garden bird bath.

37

Illus. 24. *Vase and bottle. Two unusual applications
of the mosaic technique.*

Illus. 25. The mosaicist has overcome the problem of portraying perspective and simplifying architectural forms in this mosaic of a street scene.

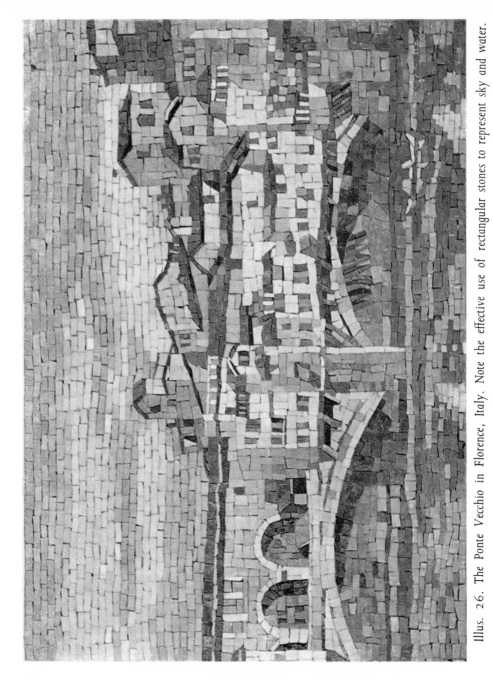

Illus. 26. The Ponte Vecchio in Florence, Italy. Note the effective use of rectangular stones to represent sky and water.

40

would be unsuitable for a mosaic that would receive punishing traffic. A foyer mosaic calls for the use of natural stone tesserae, such as marble. The range of colors available in such stones and their inherent ruggedness point up the wisdom of their use in such an application. Unpolished cubes of $\frac{3}{8}''$ marble are available in white Carrara, Bardiglio (medium grey), Rosso Verona (burnt coral), Rosa Corallo (rose coral), green Issogno, Botticino (beige), yellow Mori (ochre), yellow Sienna (deep yellow), and Belgian black.

One requirement for such a mosaic is that the floor under it must be perfectly level and not loose or weak. (A floor that moves when walked upon will soon crack the mosaic mortar and perhaps even the stones.) More important, it must be capable of supporting the added weight of stones and cement, which will be considerable even over a relatively small area.

Ideally, such a mosaic should be laid on a layer of concrete that has been placed upon the floor in the designated area and allowed to dry to form a concrete-slab base. Affix the tesserae to this, using one of the permanent adhesives; a more desirable method is to use a portland cement mortar to "butter" the backs of the individual tesserae before they are set in place on the concrete slab. A painter's palette knife makes an excellent tool for this purpose. When these are dry, fill in the spaces between tesserae by working grout into the mosaic. Finish the mosaic by polishing it with a mixture of pumice powder and water and then oil it with light mineral oil to bring out the color.

You may have to remove the baseboard skirting of the room in which this mosaic is laid so that the mosaic extends completely from wall to wall. This can be nailed back into place upon completion of the mosaic.

Illus. 27. Clown and mandolin. A perfect subject for a mosaic for a child's playroom.

Ideas for Mosaics

Let us assume that you have now made several mosaics using simple geometric patterns or elementary representational ideas. Where else can you get ideas for your mosaics? For more elaborate geometric designs, there is always the world of nature to go to. For a skiing friend, how about mosaic hot plates with snowflake designs—there are an infinite number of these and an encyclopaedia will give you some ideas as to their variety.

For a child's room, how about some simple pictures inspired by a book of nursery rhymes? If the picture you want to mosaic is not the right size for the base you have selected, it will be a simple matter to transfer it by using the method of squares shown in Illus. 28. Rule off a certain number of squares in each direction on the picture. (You can do this on clear tracing paper and lay it on the picture if you don't want to mark it up with lines.) Now draw an equal number of squares (different size boxes, of course) in each direction on the board to which you are going to fix your mosaic. Draw diagonal lines through the box corners too. You will find by drawing the content of each box (or half box) on your mosaic board in just the same fashion as in the boxes on the original drawing, you can make an exact duplicate of the picture. Try it! It's fun and a useful skill to know.

If the drawing or illustration that you are transferring is the same size as the mosaic you want, do not forget a much-neglected copying aid—ordinary carbon paper. Or use the artist's carbon-substitute: coating the back of the drawing you wish to trace with graphite from a very soft lead pencil.

Do you know someone who is interested in art appreciation? You can make some delightful mosaic gifts by copying prints of the world's great paintings onto a baseboard and turning out copies of these masterpieces in tesserae. The mosaic of Gauguin's "Tahitian Women" (Illus. 30) was made in just this fashion.

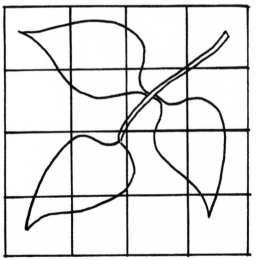

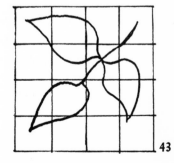

Illus. 28. Enlarging a mosaic design is easy when you use the method of squares.

Illus. 29. An Egyptian scene on a radiator-top mosaic. The choice of subject is appropriate to its "warm" location.

MAKE A RADIATOR-TOP MOSAIC

Materials Checklist

baseboard cut to cover the top of radiator (should be
    thick to overcome tendency to warp)
tesserae
mosaic cement
edging material

One of the neglected spots in most homes is the radiator top. With a mosaic, you can transform this into a decorative and utilitarian place. The only necessary precaution is that your materials (baseboard, adhesive, etc.) must be able to withstand the considerable heat to which they will be subjected.

The procedure is simple. Cut out a baseboard to a size and shape that will cover the top of your radiator. Place this on top of the radiator; on the underside of the baseboard mark the position of the parallel sections (ribs) towards each end of the radiator and in the middle. Nail three cleats to the underside of the baseboard, selecting wood that will project between the ribs of the radiator for support.

Now mosaic the top of the baseboard with an appropriate design. Fix the tesserae to the baseboard with a permanent adhesive and grout the spaces between the tesserae with thin mosaic cement. Finish off with a wood or metal edging that will not be too vulnerable to the heat of the radiator.

Representing Faces and Figures

The illustrations in this book will show you the possibilities for representing the human face and figure in mosaics. Faces and figures can be stylized, as in "Eskimo Woman" (Illus. 49) or "The Clown" (Illus. 27); others are more carefully delineated ("Maximian," Illus. 69; "Tahitian Women," Illus. 30; or "The Singing Lesson," Illus. 21).

Illus. 30. "Tahitian Women," a mosaic copy of the famous painting by Paul Gauguin. Note the interplay of light and shadow on the faces of the women and the three-dimensional modelling of the figures.

The important thing to remember is that no mosaic-making technique can approximate the detail to be achieved by paint and brush. The reproduction of the human face or figure in detail is perhaps the most challenging task to which a mosaicist can set himself. It is better not to try to reproduce a portrait realistically in the beginning, but interpret and stylize as much as possible.

MAKE A FIREPLACE-SLAB MOSAIC

Materials Checklist
marble or unglazed tile tesserae
portland cement
oak edging

A mosaic in front of your fireplace or under your heating stove will be both decorative and practical, an important consideration being that sparks or hot embers will not be able to ignite the floor boards. However, laying a mosaic on a portion of a board floor can be risky. Make certain that your floor is solid and not susceptible to movement before you begin, or a cracked and unsightly mosaic may be the end result.

First make a frame by nailing quarter-round or other appropriately shaped oak edging to the floor. (Use the 45° mitre joint at the corners where the sides of this "frame" join, as described in the section on edging.) Coat the enclosed area with a layer of portland cement as described in the project for an entrance mosaic. When this is dry, "butter" marble or ceramic tesserae with the same mortar (using your painter's palette knife) and fix them to the base slab.

Finish off by grouting the interstices between the
tesserae with a thinner mixture of the same mortar

Illus. 31. *A typical fireplace-slab mosaic. Even the mosaic seems to radiate warmth from its dancing flames. Note the neat edging framing the mosaic.*

to the height of the tesserae and the edging. If the tesserae you used were marble cubes, polish the mosaic with a mixture of pumice powder and water. Then clean the face of the mosaic and apply light mineral oil to bring out the color of the stones.

If you used ceramic or glass tesserae, clean the excess grout from the face of the mosaic, using copper scouring pads, and finish with sealer.

Direct and Indirect Methods

Up until now your mosaics have all been made by attaching them directly to a base. This is the "direct" method of making mosaics; it is the method most commonly used to make some of the world's greatest mosaics of antiquity.

There is another method of making mosaics, and you may now feel proficient enough to try your hand at it. Furthermore, it is the only practical way of covering a vertical surface with a mosaic—the individual mosaic stones will have a way of sliding out of position if you try to mosaic a vertical surface by the direct method. (Remember that in putting a mosaic on the cupboard door you removed the vertical door from its hinges and treated it as a horizontal surface.)

In the method called the indirect or "reverse" method, you first create your mosaic by drawing the design at full scale on a sheet of brown wrapping paper. This design should be drawn in reverse (flopped-over), as a mirror image of the design that you want to achieve.

When you are satisfied with the design you have drawn, fix the tesserae face down on the paper using a temporary adhesive such as flour-and-water paste. A good recipe for flour-and-water paste is this:

one part white flour
eight parts water
mix thoroughly
boil 5 minutes
strain out lumps

Be sure to place the tesserae in the exact position and relationship (reversed, of course) that you will want them to occupy in the finished mosaic and with the exact spacing between the stones that they will retain.

Then prepare a bed of relatively soft cement on the surface to which the mosaic is to be applied. Also, trowel a coating of this soft cement on the backs of the face-down paper-mounted tesserae; it will not matter if some of this cement gets into the spaces between the tesserae. Now, lift the paper carefully and press the backs of the tesserae, still on the paper, into the cement bed. You must be careful to press hard enough against the paper and uniformly all over to force the cement into the spaces between the tesserae.

TIP: Use an old-fashioned kitchen rolling pin to ensure even pressure and good adhesion. This is an especially good tool if the surface to be covered with the mosaic is a curved one, as for example a concrete column.

When the cement bed has begun to set (in about a half hour or so), then and only then, moisten the paper with a sponge and carefully peel it from the face of the mosaic. Do not become alarmed if some of the tesserae seem to have shifted slightly out of place; this is to be expected. Some adjustment of the tesserae can always be made if the paper peeling is done before the mortar has set too hard. Tesserae can also be tamped into place by laying a flat board on the surface and tapping it lightly with a mallet or hammer.

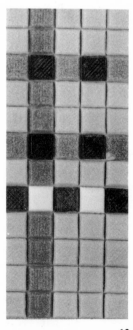

The reverse or indirect method is excellent for making mosaics using glass tesserae or natural stone—materials where the color pervades the tesserae from front to back. However, ceramic and porcelain tesserae have their color only on the face and consequently do not lend themselves to the making of mosaics by the indirect method. Unless you have had considerable experience in making mosaics, it will be impossible for you to follow the progress of the creation of a mosaic using ceramic or porcelain tesserae pasted face down on the design paper, for the tile backs of the tesserae all look the same.

It is possible, however, to add an extra step in order to use the reverse or indirect method in such cases. Draw the design on a sheet of brown wrapping paper exactly as it will appear in the finished mosaic (i.e., not reversed). First create the mosaic by pasting the tesserae into position face up on this paper, using a temporary adhesive like flour-and-water paste. When you are satisfied with the design and layout and when the stones are thoroughly dry in position on this paper, coat the faces of the tesserae with the same flour-and-water paste and paste still another sheet of plain brown wrapping paper into position on top of the stones. What you will have when this is dry is a "sandwich" of tesserae between two sheets of paper. The mosaic should now be turned over very carefully so that the paper with the design is on top.

TIP: Use two sheets of cardboard to hold the mosaic "sandwich" while you turn it.

Now moisten the paper on the backs of the stones with a sponge and carefully peel it off. You are now at the same stage that you would have been if you had pasted the stones face down on a sheet of paper. From this point you can proceed as described before.

In order to avoid the necessity of working with paper of unwieldly size in the indirect method, you can cut the paper into smaller segments, once the stones are affixed face down on the paper. Be sure that you cut irregularly-shaped segments where

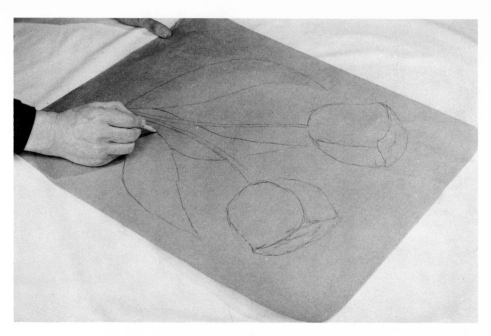

Illus. 32. (Above) Making a mosaic for a table top by the indirect method. First, sketch the design on a sheet of brown wrapping paper. Illus. 33. (Below) Use a temporary adhesive to glue the tesserae face down on the design.

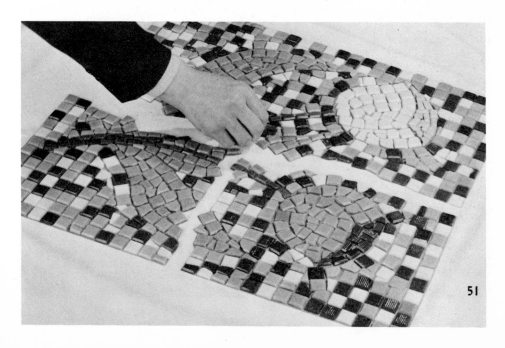

Illus. 34. (Above) The design takes shape as you glue the last of the tesserae into place. Illus. 35. (Below) After cutting the brown wrapping paper into four segments, lay the individual sheets into place in their bed of mosaic cement.

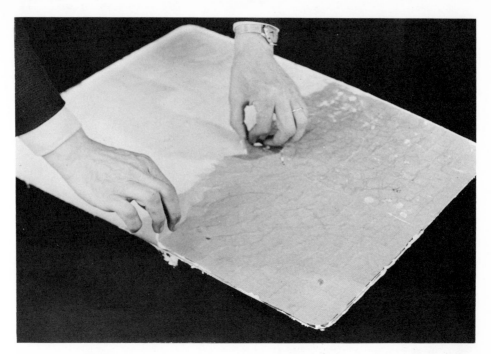

Illus. 36. (Above) When the mosaic cement has set, remove the paper backing. Note how the paper is peeled back upon itself. Illus. 37. (Below) The finished table with mosaic top. The dark plastic edging has been fastened to the mosaic baseboard with contrasting brass escutcheon pins.

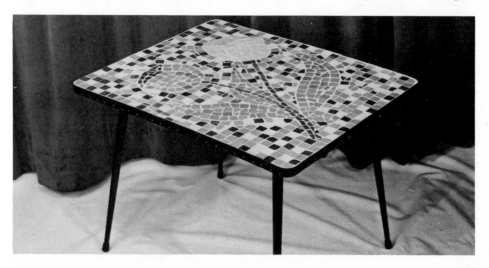

possible. This will avoid a too-regular pattern of joints when the sheets of paper are finally affixed to the cement bed. The bed should only be prepared in small areas to receive the segments that can be applied in a single working session. Do not cement an entire wall unless you are prepared to mosaic it at the same time. It is always better to work in small sections to achieve the best holding qualities of the freshly applied cement.

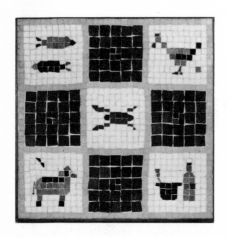

MAKE A MOSAIC FOR YOUR KITCHEN WALL

Materials Checklist
tesserae
mosaic cement (plaster of Paris is suitable here)

Illus. 38. Mosaic motifs for a kitchen wall. Note the clever intermixing of $\frac{3}{4}$" by $\frac{3}{4}$" stones and $\frac{3}{8}$" by $\frac{3}{8}$" stones.

Using the indirect method, you can now make a mosaic and apply it to your kitchen wall. Such a mosaic using appropriate motifs will help to brighten up a kitchen. For motifs, choose subjects like cooking utensils or fruits and vegetables. Simplify them or even stylize them.

Once the design has been prepared and pasted on brown wrapping paper, you should prepare the wall to receive the mosaic. Scrape away any paint and outside plaster within the area of the mosaic. Be sure that you get down to the sandy rough plaster or to the lathing for a good solid foundation to which your

54

mosaic can adhere. Moisten the area well with water and apply a smooth layer of the mosaic cement you have selected. Let it dry for a day or two before proceeding to mount your mosaic on the wall.

Now coat this prepared area with fresh mosaic cement, after first moistening it. (Always moisten an area to which mosaic cement is to be applied; otherwise the "old" mortar would draw moisture from the fresh cement applied to it and cause an imperfect bond.) Also coat the backs of the tesserae mounted on the brown paper and press them into the cement bed. Press them tight with a flat board or roll them with an old-fashioned rolling pin. When the mosaic cement has begun to set (in about a half hour if you are using plaster of Paris as your mosaic cement) peel off the brown paper by moistening it with a sponge and peeling it back upon itself, not out from the wall. Fill in any remaining open spaces with a thinner grouting mixture of the same cement. Complete the mosaic by cleaning it with copper scouring pads and sealing with sealer and wax.

Illus. 39. An ambitious project: A pictorial mosaic for a fireplace wall.

Illus. 40. Putting up an outside mosaic. The top segment of the mosaic has already been placed in its bed of cement. The mosaicist is plastering the wall with a layer of mosaic cement to receive the next segment.

Illus. 41. A segment of the mosaic pasted on paper now receives a coating of mosaic cement.

Illus. 42. This segment, coated with mosaic cement is placed in its bed of mosaic cement. Care must be exercised so that the edges of the joint match up exactly with the adjoining segment.

56

Illus. 43. After being moistened, the sheets of paper backing up the mosaic segment are removed by peeling it back upon itself.

Illus. 44. The mosaicist is finishing off one section of the outside mosaic by grouting any empty spaces between mosaic stones with a thin mixture of mosaic cement.

Other Locations for Mosaics

By now you will undoubtedly have begun to think of other places where you can apply mosaics. If you have an outside terrace, it can be made more attractive with a "mosaic" of large, flat, colored stones in a bed of concrete. Perhaps you will want to enclose an old-fashioned bathtub or bathroom sink in a plywood frame and apply a mosaic to it. A dark corner of any room can be brightened with the light reflected from a picture-framed mosaic of bright bits of mirror glass.

Illus. 45. A mosaic for a window sill can brighten an unusual location.
Illus. 46. (Right, above) Coating the composition hardboard with a layer of waterproofing compound. The next step will be to apply a layer of mosaic cement into which the paper bearing the mosaic will be set. Finally, the paper will be removed.

MAKE A WINDOW-SILL MOSAIC

Materials Checklist
sheet of composition hardboard
  (masonite) the size of window sill
mastic cement
permanent adhesive
mosaic cement
edging material

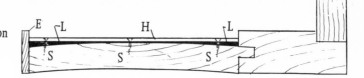

Illus. 47. It may be
necessary to mount a
baseboard of composition
hardboard on the
window sill if it is
badly warped. (L)
layer of mastic (H)
panel of composition
hardboard (E) wood
edging strip, and (S)
flat-headed screws
countersunk to hold
hardboard panel.

A mosaic on a window sill will combine beauty
and practicality; a window sill protected by a mosaic
is less likely to be damaged by rain coming through a
window accidentally left open.

A window ledge is usually a separate piece of wood
set directly into the window frame or casing. If the
wood is not warped, the mosaic can be set directly
on to the window ledge. If the ledge is warped, it is
desirable to fix a sheet of composition hardboard
(masonite) of the same size to the window sill to
serve as the base for the mosaic. If it is uneven, the sill
can be planed down before mounting the composition
hardboard. Apply a thick coat of mastic (such as is
used to mount plastic floor tile) or other cushioning
adhesive between the sill and the composition board
before screwing it to the surface; this will serve to
level off any irregularities in the sill surface.

When the composition board has been mounted,
glue a thin wood edging to the window ledge,
letting it project above the composition hardboard
to the finished height of the mosaic.

The mosaic can now be laid into place by the direct
or indirect method.

Illus. 48. First lay out
the design of the
window-sill mosaic on a
sheet of ruled paper upon
which the tesserae will
later be affixed using
temporary adhesive.

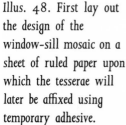

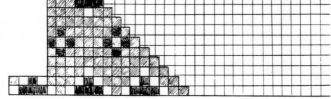

Other Objects for Mosaics

Illus. 49. *A stylized motif, such as this figure of an Eskimo woman, makes an excellent decoration for a wall plaque.*

The mosaicist should always be on the look-out for suitable objects to serve as bases for mosaics. Every dish, vase, bottle or other container is a potential subject for decoration with a mosaic. Bottles and other vessels with narrow necks should be decorated externally; wide-mouthed vessels can be decorated inside and outside. A simple pottery flower pot, for example, decorated with mosaics becomes a beautiful work of art.

TIP: Always sketch your design on the vessel with a crayon or grease pencil to determine the suitability of size and subject before proceeding to add your mosaic.

Pottery vessels should always be wetted down thoroughly before being coated with mosaic cement—otherwise they will absorb water from the mortar and make a poor bond.

On most curved or irregular surfaces, it is always advisable to use small chips rather than full-sized tesserae—the small pieces make it easier to follow the configuration of the surface.

TIP: To hold mosaics to vases, bottles and similar objects, mosaic a portion (a horizontal band) at a time, starting from the bottom and working up. Tie a woman's discarded nylon stocking around the object to hold the stones in place and to keep them from slipping downwards in the mosaic cement bed.

MAKE A MOSAIC ON A BOTTLE

Materials Checklist
bottle (champagne or soda—the shape will be recognizable)
portland cement
tesserae
mosaic cement
lamp hardware (if you intend to make a lamp base)

A bottle will make an unusual base for a decorative mosaic. Unfortunately, glass can be an extremely fragile foundation for a mosaic. There is a way around this, however: Pour a portland cement mixture into the bottle to be covered with a mosaic, filling it completely. Now wait for several days. When the cement has hardened completely, carefully break away the bottle, being careful not to cut yourself on the broken glass. The resultant cement casting of the original bottle will be a perfect base for applying your mosaic.

You can easily make a bottle into an attractive lamp base in a similar fashion. Get a brass rod as high as your lamp will be tall. The upper end of the rod should be threaded to receive the necessary sockets and lamp-shade hardware, which are procurable in a hardware store. Plug up the unthreaded end of the brass rod with modelling clay and plunge it all the way to the bottom of the cement-filled bottle soon after pouring in the cement.

When the cement has dried, break away the bottle and apply your mosaic to the cement casting. Remove the clay plug from the bottom of the brass tubing and run a lamp cord up through the tube. A pull-chain socket or other switch and an appropriate lamp shade will complete the project.

When covering the cement bottle casting with a mosaic, be sure to start at the bottom and work upwards. Settling the mosaic stones in their bed of mosaic cement should be no problem—just roll the bottle on the table top like a rolling pin and the stones will become seated firmly. It will probably be advisable to mosaic the portland cement bottle in stages, allowing each horizontal band to dry thoroughly before applying the next layer.

Illus. 50. Two unusual objects for mosaic application: The fruit dish and the wide-mouthed jar have been made more attractive and colorful through the technique of the mosaic.

Unusual Mosaic Materials

Illus. 51. (Left) This mosaic was made entirely of stones collected by the mosaicist during an afternoon's walk.

Illus. 52. (Right) A tea pot, broken accidentally, has not gone to waste. This unusual mosaic was made with the fragments—a lively rooster against a rough concrete background.

The true mosaicist never considers that his mosaic materials are limited to natural stones or man-made imitations. Seeds, fruit stones and pips of all kinds provide material for an unusual kind of mosaic. Beans, lima beans, kidney beans, dried peas, coffee beans and lentils – all can contribute their distinctive shapes, textures and colors.

No longer should broken dishes or chinaware be

consigned to the scrap heap. Let your friends know that you are collecting unusual mosaic materials and you will soon be deluged with usable materials of every sort.

If you have any familiarity with ceramics, you may even wish to make your own glazed ceramic tesserae: Flatten a slab of clay with a rolling pin until it is the desired thickness (about $\frac{3}{8}''$ will be about right). Glaze it with a commercial, colored ceramic glaze. In about two hours you will be able to cut the glazed clay slab into tesserae. The tesserae must be air-dried for several days and then should be fired in a kiln at a temperature of $1,850°$ F. When cutting your tesserae, remember that you are by no means restricted to square or rectangular shapes—you can cut any shape from the clay before firing.

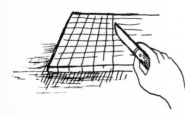

You can also make your own colored plaster of Paris tesserae easily at home. Coat a glass plate with soapy water or petroleum jelly to keep the plaster of Paris from sticking to the glass. Mix plaster of Paris in a large tin. Have some smaller tins on hand and some water-soluble or powdered pigment dyes. Add the dyes to the plaster in the individual cans. Now spread the colored plaster of Paris individually on the glass plate so that it is about $\frac{3}{8}''$ thick. When the plaster starts to become firm, cut it into tesserae with a sharp knife.

You can also make plaster of Paris tesserae in square or rectangular shapes by using old ice-cube trays to mold the tesserae, a dozen at a time. The plaster of Paris can be colored in the same fashion during the mixing process, using water-soluble dyes or colored pigments. Remember that plaster of Paris is highly absorbent; if you make a mosaic using plaster of Paris tesserae, sealing with silicone sealer or white shellac is an absolute necessity.

Illus. 53. *A mosaic can be made of dried peas, beans and even coffee beans, individually placed by hand upon the design.*

MAKE A MOSAIC FROM FOOD

Materials Checklist
peas, kidney beans, coffee beans, lima beans, seeds, and other miscellaneous materials from the kitchen
baseboard (try artist's canvas board)
adhesive

Here is a project that will challenge your ingenuity and your skill at improvisation. The object is to make a mosaic using various seeds (peas, beans, etc.) and similar food materials found in the kitchen.

Take a piece of light cardboard. Sketch your design on the cardboard—perhaps you can make this into a decorative mosaic for your kitchen using kitchen motifs as well as kitchen materials! Now, as in the first gravel mosaic that you made, coat each area of your design with an adhesive (such as flour-and-water paste) and mount peas, beans, sunflower seeds, herbs, etc.—anything that you find in the kitchen, chosen for its color, texture, size or shape. When you are done, you will have a mosaic that is truly unusual.

If you used flour and water as the adhesive, in a pinch you could even eat your mosaic! Because of the nature of the materials used, such a mosaic would be an intriguing and perfectly harmless project for even the smallest child. **65**

The Importance of Backgrounds

As you have progressed in mastering the art of the mosaic, you have undoubtedly come to appreciate the effect of the size of the stones you select on the over-all mosaic. Similarly, the relationship of the design motif and the background is also important. The background can be restful or jumpy, it can serve as a balance for the central motif, or it can weaken its effect. Generally speaking, the background should be simple and uniform in color.

Illustrations 54 to 58 show several backgrounds with square stones or cut stones. The type of background you select will depend on your own taste and the emphasis you wish to make on the motif itself. By arranging small square stones along symmetrical lines, you will achieve a restful and unobtrusive background. If you want to give your mosaic life and originality, arrange them along diverging, converging or broken lines. Square stones will have to be shaped where they adjoin the outline of the motif.

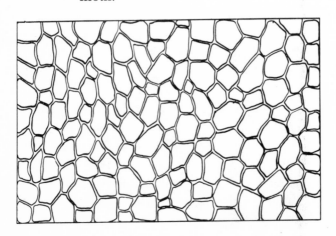

Illus. 54. An interesting over-all "random" effect can be achieved by using broken tesserae or irregular pebbles.

Illus. 55. Varying the shapes and placement of tesserae.

Illustrations 56 and 57 show two different ways of composing a mosaic; in both cases the motif represents a bird on a branch. Note how the arrangement of the background can alter the general effect. In both cases, the background consists of $\frac{3}{4}''$ by $\frac{3}{4}''$ stones, but in Illus. 56 they have been laid diagonally according to a strictly symmetrical pattern.

The composition of such a mosaic must always start with the motif. The stones, and chiefly those representing the bird's feathers should be finely cut. The effect of the wings and tail will be heightened by the use of many colors. Once the motif has been laid down, the stones adjoining it should be cut carefully and then the background should be laid in.

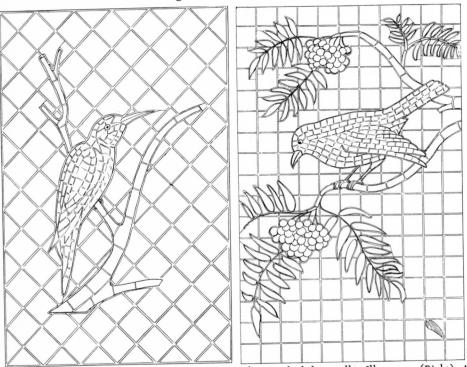

Illus. 56. (Left) A bird motif on a background of stones laid diagonally. Illus. 57. (Right) A similar motif against a different background of the same stones. Note the effect achieved by changing the background.

At the bottom right corner of Illus. 57 can be seen a small leaf. The illustration shows clearly how a ¾″ by ¾″ stone should be cut to achieve the desired shape. Illus. 58 represents a fish against a background of ⅜″ by ⅜″ stones. Note the wavy effect of the background, which suggests movement and is particularly suited for portraying running water.

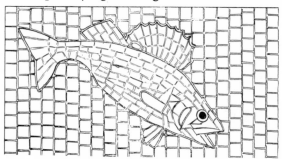

Illus. 58. This background is effective for representing water. Although the stones are laid in vertical bands, there is an uneven, wavy effect that gives the impression of water.

Colored Cements and Grouts

The mosaicist is not limited to the use of white or near-white cement in his mosaics. When experience in the handling of mosaic materials has been achieved, you may wish to consider the use of mosaic cement of more than one color in filling the interstices of a mosaic on the theory that the spaces between the stones in a sense contribute to the over-all effect of a mosaic in quite the same way as do the tesserae.

If it can be said of any art form, it can be said that mosaics are perhaps more susceptible to inventiveness and ingenuity in the finding of materials and in the methods of their application to surfaces than is any other art form. As a mosaicist, you will only really be limited in what you attempt by your own imagination.

How Mosaics Developed

Mosaics are truly as old as time. What you have been doing in the successive projects in this book is not unlike the progression that has taken place in the art of the mosaic through the years. Undoubtedly, now that you are an accomplished mosaicist (but still with much to learn) you will want to know something about the manner in which the mosaic developed.

"Mosaic," as a word probably is derived from the Greek *mouseios*, which means "belonging to the muses." A mosaic is defined as a pattern of small pieces of differently colored materials placed close together so as to form a surface. The mosaic can be considered an outgrowth of the ancient decorative art of inlaying. As the area of the inlay became greater, the original material became merely a base and a frame to hold the pieces of inlay.

Historically, it is difficult to draw a sharp line between inlays which are not mosaics and true mosaics, but the mosaic was in use in Mesopotamia at least as early as 5000-4000 B.C. Among the debris of houses of the al 'Ubaid period in southern Mesopotamia have been found cones of baked clay, shaped somewhat like a pencil, with the blunt end painted red or black or left uncolored. These were used in wall mosaics, and apparently were cone-shaped to facilitate their being embedded in a matrix. The elements used in these earliest mosaics were simple: zigzags, triangles and lozenges. In time, animal motifs were added to the geometric motifs.

The background materials of the Mesopotamian mosaics have long since disintegrated, but they are said by Sir Leonard Woolley to have been a kind of colored plaster.

The Sumerians of ancient Babylonia also decorated various objects—harps, game boards and furniture—with silhouetted figures cut from the solid portion of conch shells and set against a mosaic background of pieces of lapis lazuli. The most famous example is perhaps the remarkable "Standard of Ur," with rows of men and animals portraying a field of battle and the subsequent victory celebration—all in mosaic.

Work that can be described as mosaic existed in early Egypt, although it was largely confined to the minor arts. Numerous objects show bits of colored glass, lapis lazuli and other stones inlaid into small

Illus. 59. This Roman rabbit sitting amidst mushrooms dates from the 1st century B.C., yet it could have been made yesterday. The mosaic is composed of glass tesserae.

71

Illus. 60. Captured in a marble Roman mosaic dating from the time of Christ, a pair of ducks watch over their brood of ducklings.

compartments of ivory, usually on a miniature scale. Similar work on a larger scale appears as architectural decoration in the lower Nile regions.

The early Minoans of ancient Greece were also familiar with mosaic. Sir Arthur Evans found a rough stone box in the Lesser Palace at Knossos containing small tesserae of crystal, amethyst, beryl, lapis lazuli and even solid gold, indicating that they must have been used for very fine work. For pavements, the Minoans embedded pebbles in hard clay, often using different colors to form simple patterns.

In Mohammedan countries, the art of the small-scale geometric inlay of wood, often combined with mother-of-pearl and ivory, was developed to a fine degree for the decoration of furniture and decorative panels. The Mohammedans never imitated the cube mosaics of the Roman or Byzantine type and the few examples of Mohammedan mosaics in this style

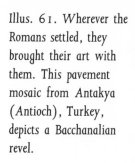

Illus. 61. Wherever the Romans settled, they brought their art with them. This pavement mosaic from Antakya (Antioch), Turkey, depicts a Bacchanalian revel.

such as "The Dome in the Rock" at Jerusalem, the great Mosque at Damascus, or the Mosque at Cordova in Spain, all turn out to have been done by early Christians or Byzantines.

Of course, the Mohammedans had no need to imitate, for they had the great ceramic traditions of ancient Mesopotamia and Persia to draw upon and from these traditions came their justly-famous wall tiles. Persian ceramic workers developed a mosaic method and tiles, which from the 14th to the 17th centuries were used in some of the most beautiful polychrome decorations. The technique consisted of cutting large tiles of solid colors into small shaped units, which were then assembled into complex patterns. The predominant color was a deep blue, with turquoise used for contrast, while other colors— light emerald, saffron, a rich black, and intense white —were employed for outlines and accents. The

73

patterns incorporated all of the intricacy and finesse of the work of the Persian miniature painters. Unfortunately, these beautiful mosaic tiles were supplanted by tiles of painted *faïence* and the art became a lost one.

A technique related to mosaic was called *opus sectile* by the Romans and was much used by them. It consisted of an inlay in which the materials were cut to fit the contours of the design; it was revived in the Florentine *intarsia* of the 16th and 17th centuries. This technique was perhaps most beautifully developed under the Moguls in India in their magnificent buildings at Agra (including the Taj Mahal) and Delhi, where intricate patterns are formed in cut marble while the color is furnished by inlaid colored pieces of marble and by precious and semi-precious stones.

Mosaics also played an important role in the early

Illus. 62. *Another Roman pavement mosaic from Antioch now in the Metropolitan Museum of Art in New York: The head of Spring is surrounded by a wide band of geometric shapes.*

civilizations of the New World. Included in the booty of the first Spanish conquistadores of Central America and Mexico were shields, helmets, statuettes, and other objects covered with exquisite mosaics. Although turquoise predominates in these, other materials were used—jadeite, malachite, quartz, beryl, garnet, obsidian, marcasite, gold, bits of colored shell and mother-of-pearl. These materials were fixed in a base of wood or stone or even gold or shell or pottery, and were held in place by a vegetable pitch or gum. Designs formed of the pieces were less important than the over-all effect of rich vibrant color; some of the plaques have simple patterns of concentric circles and other basic geometric motifs. What is so remarkable about these Aztec mosaics is that the stones used were roughly square or rectangular in shape and are similar to those used in Roman and early Christian mosaics. The Aztec mosaics have their origins in early Mayan civilizations, and there is every evidence that these cultures of the New World and the Old World had no contact, which makes their similarity of appearance all the more remarkable.

The Aztecs also adorned garments, weapons of war and religious objects with mosaics composed of tiny bits of feathers applied to wood, skin or paper with glue. Most such feather mosaics have not survived. It is interesting to note that the Chinese—a whole ocean away from Central America—also produced mosaics of feathers.

In Roman pavements the tesserae were usually of marble, with other stones employed only occasionally. This tended to restrict the tone range to black, white, red, yellow and olive brown. In many of the Roman pavements the tesserae were closely fitted together, giving a strikingly modern appearance to the work. Cubes of glass enamel and even gold were

Illus. 63. *After the fall of the western Roman Empire to the barbarians, the Adriatic city of Ravenna became a seat of Byzantine culture. Here in the middle of the 5th century A.D. was erected in the form of a Latin cross the now-empty mausoleum of Galla Placidia. The predominantly blue mosaics are lit by alabaster windows; this mosaic portrays the Good Shepherd.*

sometimes employed in wall decorations, as in certain fountain niches at Pompeii. Some of the pavements represent only a single geometric design, while others are truly carpets of stone with exceptionally beautiful decorative patterns. The jewel of all Roman mosaics is without a doubt the floor mosaic of "A Faun's House" at Pompeii. This measures 9 by 16 feet and consists of more than a million and a half minute marble fragments of all colors. A remarkable battle scene, it probably dates from the second century B.C. It can now be seen in the National Museum in Naples.

The art of the mosaic reached its greatest glory in the classical and early Christian mosaics of southern Europe and the Near and Middle East. Nearly all of the early classical mosaics that have survived are pavements composed of tesserae of variously colored marbles, and this has led art historians to believe that mosaics in pavements were more common than wall mosaics. With the beginning of an officially recognized Church or Christian art in the 4th century A.D., however, wall mosaics began to take on a greater importance. They differ, too, from the pavements in being composed almost entirely of tesserae of colored glass. Although the mosaic pavements continued to be made, they followed the traditional designs and techniques.

Because of their almost infinite color possibilities, mosaics have never really been equalled as architectural adornment. In the early Christian period and through the greater part of the Middle Ages in the Byzantine Empire and in Italy, they were the chief wall decoration, frescoes (paintings on plaster) being in a decidedly secondary place.

The art of the wall mosaic grew from modest beginnings in early Christian times to a glorious culmination in the 5th and 6th centuries at Constantinople, and at Ravenna, outpost of the Byzantine

Illus. 64. The Church of St. Apollinare Nuovo in Ravenna dates from the early 6th century A.D., and was built by the Emperor Theodoric. In the upper part of this mosaic are 13 scenes from the life of Christ; below, a procession of saints led by the Three Wise Men for the adoration of the Christ Child.

Empire in Italy between the 4th and 7th centuries. A second period of magnificence followed in the 12th and 13th centuries in Greece, Venice, Sicily and Rome. Unlike the stained glass windows developed as religious decoration in the northern latitudes and which depend for their effect upon flooding sunlight, mosaics are ideally suited for relatively dimly lit interiors or constantly changing surfaces, such as the curves and arches of an apse. In fact, their shimmering surfaces cannot take light which is too direct or too intense.

As for the makers of the great mosaics, interestingly, no work of mosaic art is signed by the artist before the 13th century. Perhaps this is because no other art form lends itself quite so admirably to execution by more than one person. We know that many early mosaics were often done by groups of artists.

How were the great wall mosaics made? Through the years, the techniques did not vary much. The surface to be decorated—be it wall, vault or interior of a cupola—was roughened and covered with a coat of cement. Upon this foundation, when dry, a second coat of cement was applied, and sometimes even a third coat. The direct method was used, and we find that a problem still with us today plagued the early mosaicists: Because of the comparatively rapid drying time of cement, only as much of the final coat could be laid down as would remain soft to receive the tesserae.

The best mortar was considered to be a mixture of powdered marble, lime and a natural cement. The Romans used a volcanic rock they called *pozzolana*, which has cement-like qualities. Towards the end of the 16th century, Muziano da Brescia, director of mosaic work in St. Peter's Cathedral, invented a slow-drying cement—a sort of mastic made with oil.

Illus. 65. The Basilica of San Vitale in Ravenna is considered to be the most beautiful example of Byzantine art in Europe. It was consecrated by the Archbishop Maximian in A.D. 547.

It has been demonstrated that in the best mosaic work to stand the test of time, the cement base coats are relatively thin. When executed correctly, mosaics are almost indestructible and merit the description that 15th century fresco painter and mosaicist Domenico Ghirlandaio is said to have given them: "La pittura per l'eternita."

The cement surface being ready, the tesserae were inserted into it individually so that the cement was pushed up into the space between tesserae. (This cement was often colored later if its whiteness

Illus. 66. The Archbishop Maximian, shown in this mosaic procession with the Emperor Justinian, was not in the best of health and died before this mosaic in the Basilica of San Vitale was completed. (See detail of Maximian's face on Page 85.)

interfered with the total effect.) Tesserae were roughly square or rectangular—measuring up to $\frac{3}{4}''$ on a side. The smallest stones were used in faces, hands and details, while the larger sizes were reserved for backgrounds and broad areas. Often tesserae were tilted in the mosaic bed at an angle—usually about 30°—to avoid over-reflection of light. Stones of lighter color were left in a slightly raised position above those of darker hue; blacks and dark tones were always more deeply set than the rest, indicating that the early mosaicists had a clear understanding of the problems of illumination and tone values.

The glass used in the manufacture of tesserae was usually colored by the addition of metallic oxides. Oxide of tin was used to make a color opaque. Copper oxide was employed to give blues, chromium oxide for the greens, etc. Gold and silver glass stones were also manufactured, the color being applied to the front of a clear glass stone and protected by a fused glass film. About the 8th century, the colorless glass base of gold tesserae was supplanted by a base of red glass for a richer effect.

In the earliest mosaics, the backgrounds are usually light, and marble tesserae may even have been used with the glass tesserae. Blue backgrounds were used as early as the 4th century and maintained a certain popularity. In the 5th century and the early 6th century, the use of gold backgrounds was introduced and became almost universal.

The range of colors employed in wall mosaics was never very large. In the nave of the church of St. Maria Maggiore in Rome there are only 48 different tones comprising shades of red, blue, rose, green, yellow, and grey, in addition to black and brown. The number was varied from mosaic to mosaic, but in the best work only a comparatively few strong colors were used. It was only when mosaic art tried to imitate the methods and the look of painting that gradations of tone were multiplied. The Vatican's mosaic studio, which is charged with the care and restoration of mosaics there, can even today boast that it carries 28,000 different shades in stock.

Thomas Whittemore, in a monumental 1933 study

Illus. 67. Constantinople was the seat of the Byzantine Empire. The mosaics that have survived are of a later date than those at Ravenna. Here a reverent Emperor John Comenus and Empress Irene offer gifts to Mary and Jesus in this 12-th century mosaic in the south gallery of Santa Sophia.

of the mosaics of St. Sophia in Istanbul, has recorded the colors employed. For example, among the marble tesserae used in the narthex, he found a white and a neutral tint, yellow ochre, yellow brown, cadmium orange, rose madder and Rubens madder. Glass tesserae colors included lemon yellow, red ochre, red brown, indigo, purple lake, Van Dyke brown, rose brown, raw umber, burnt umber, cobalt blue, ultra-marine veridian, cobalt green, chrome yellow, chrome green, and hematite black. If some of the most splendid mosaics the world has ever seen could have been made with such a limited "palette" of colors, the mosaicist of today should not feel that a large assortment of tones is required before he can begin work.

There is some question as to how much of the actual design of early mosaics was indicated on the surface as a guide for the placement of the tesserae. In some cases, plaster may have been laid on the cement base and the elements of the design drawn and colored upon this. It seems to have been more usual for the design to have been scratched on the cement, with the larger areas of color indicated as a guide. Originally, mosaicists worked from drawings; as the influence of painters increased, elaborate designs were provided on paper for the mosaicist to follow. It was only a small step to paste the stones directly on the paper and then to cut this up into sections and mount them in place. Thus, the indirect method was born.

The cement that showed between the tesserae was sometimes stained to blend with the colors of the stones themselves; alternatively it was left a neutral grey. With backgrounds of gold tesserae, it was common to stain the cement red to heighten the richness of the effect.

Today's mosaicist can even profit from the mistakes

Illus. 68. This mosaic over the St. Alipio portal of the Basilica of St. Mark in Venice was once threatened with damage by gunfire. Dating from the latter part of the 13th century, it shows the transferral of the remains of St. Mark, patron saint of Venice, from Alexandria to the Basilica. A 1648 decree put a stop to cannon salutes in the Piazza of St. Mark's.

of the past. In the restoration of the triumphal arch of St. Maria Maggiore at Rome, a work of the 5th century, it was discovered that the 2-inch-thick foundation coat of cement had been applied to a perfectly smooth brick wall to which it had not bound sufficiently. Also, the surface coat of cement in which the tesserae were embedded had in places separated from the foundation coat. The surface was removed in pieces and the foundation was restored before replacing the surface.

TIP: Always make sure that your mosaic is firmly bonded to the base or baseboard.

83

In the 13th-century apse of this same church, it was discovered that Jacopo Torriti, the mosaicist, had studded the foundation cement with iron nails to strengthen it. These nails have now rusted away. Not only have they stained the surface of the mosaic, but they have caused the cement to disintegrate.

TIP: Never add adulterants to your mosaic materials.

In 1648, a decree was passed in Venice forbidding the discharge of cannon salutes and fireworks in the Piazza of St. Mark's because it was found that the vibrations were causing damage to the mosaics in the basilica.

TIP: Vibration of any kind—even from ordinary sources—can damage a mosaic. Give your mosaics a solid foundation.

The Renaissance, which brought about such remarkable changes in architecture, in sculpture and in painting dealt the mosaic art a death blow. In order to survive at all, the mosaic became the slave and the imitator of painting. Many of the simple secrets of the early mosaicists were forgotten as artists tried to make stone do what it never was intended to do. They forgot that mosaics are essentially architectural decoration and, as such, should be in scale and in character with their surroundings. The inevitable result was that the mosaics and the buildings decorated with them suffered from their misapplication. Sir Christopher Wren in the 17th century had toyed with the idea of employing mosaics in St. Paul's Cathedral in London, but it was never carried through. The decline continued, and throughout the 18th century the only workshops where the mosaic art survived were those of Venice and Rome.

At the beginning of the 19th century, a revival of interest in the Middle Ages and a new spirit of

Illus. 69. Detail of the face of the Archbishop Maximian from the mosaic in the Basilica of San Vitale in Ravenna. (See Illus. 66.) Note how well the mosaicist has captured the Archbishop's sickness-ravaged features.

architecture brought renewed hope for the mosaic. Many old mosaics were restored during this time— and what was missing from a mosaic was often supplied by over-enthusiastic mosaicists to the distress and confusion of today's art historians.

It remained for the 20th century in both Europe and America to usher in the beginning of a new renaissance for the mosaic. Increasingly, mosaics found their way into religious edifices and public buildings. Following the end of World War II, the art of the mosaic entered an entirely new realm. Instead of being something esoteric carried on by specialists, it became the province of the amateur, the craftsman who saw in it a neglected avenue of expression, one combining the twin objectives of beauty and practicality.

All over the world, thousands of people have chosen mosaics as a hobby, to occupy their leisure and to help them to escape from the daily routine of a life which affords less and less opportunity for the personal development and expression of the individual.

The materials of the mosaicist have been little changed with time; they have only been refined. The techniques of the mosaic have been changed not at all, and the mechanical and artistic problems that face today's mosaicist are the same as were solved by the now-forgotten mosaicists of the Vatican, Venice, Ravenna, Constantinople and even earlier. Few art forms can offer such a link with the past. In this unchanging nature of the art perhaps lies the challenge and attraction of the mosaic: It is at the same time one of the newest of the art forms and one of the oldest.

Illus. 70. The mosaic in the modern world. Here mosaics serve as a
background for a display of dresses in a department store window.

Index

cy 2

738.5
ARV

Arvois, Edmond
Making mosaics

Date Due

NOV 24 8			

You can start to make mosaics practically from the first page as you transform a plain bowl into a mosaic candy dish. With easy-to-follow instructions, you find short cuts for creating mosaics from readily available materials using simple tools. Begins with simple objects and progresses into ambitious projects.